Tickle-Toe Rhymes

Tickle-Toe Rhymes

Joan Knight
Pictures by John Wallner

COLLINS

William Collins Sons & Co Ltd
London · Glasgow · Sydney · Auckland
Toronto · Johannesburg

Originally published in the United States by
Orchard Books, 387 Park Avenue South, New York,
New York 10016

First published in the UK in 1990 by
William Collins Sons & Co Ltd

Text copyright © 1989 Joan Knight
Illustrations © 1989 John Wallner

A CIP catalogue record for this book is available
from the British Library

ISBN 0 00 195964 6

Printed and bound in Portugal by Resopal

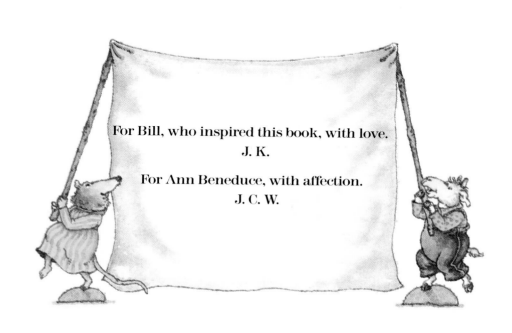

For Bill, who inspired this book, with love.
J. K.

For Ann Beneduce, with affection.
J. C. W.

One little piggy wore leggings,
Two little piggies wore wigs,
Three little piggies wore bustles,
Four little piggies did jigs,
Five little piggies wore nothing at all
And said that the others were prigs.

One little kid took a limo,
Two little kids took a bus,
Three little kids took a buggy,
Four little kids made a fuss,
Five little kids created a stir
Crying, "Nanny, what about *us*?"

One little bunny grew carrots,
Two little bunnies grew greens,
Three little bunnies grew mushrooms,
Four little bunnies grew beans,
Five little bunnies pickled them all
And served them in cabbage tureens.

One little hippo brought a blanket,
Two little hippos brought ham,
Three little hippos made lemonade,
Four little hippos spread jam,
Five little hippos said lunch was over
And they all hopped back in the pram.

One little skunk smelled of violets,
Two little skunks smelled of stew,
Three little skunks smelled horrid,
Four little skunks said, "Phew!"
Five little skunks smelled delicious –
Just the way you do, too!

One little monkey laughed loudly,
Two little monkeys nearly burst,
Three little monkeys laughed at others,
Four little monkeys did worse,
Five little monkeys wept crocodile tears
Into an alligator purse.

One little grizzly grew grumpy,
Two little grizzlies grew grim,
Three little grizzlies grew testy,
Four little grizzlies were prim,
Five little grizzlies found some porridge
And filled up their bowls to the brim.

One little beaver worked hard as can be,
Two little beavers worked more,
Three little beavers worked side by side,
Four little beavers were sore,
Five little beavers packed a picnic lunch
And spent the day at the shore.

One little tiger had a tantrum,
Two little tigers had a row,
Three little tigers had a pillow fight,
Four little tigers took a bow,
Five little tigers, feeling cranky,
Said, "Enough is enough for now!"

One little panda read music,
Two little pandas read Poe,
Three little pandas read recipes,
Four little pandas made dough,
Five little pandas put ear muffs on
And went out to play in the snow.

One little possum ate a parsnip,
Two little possums ate some beet,
Three little possums ate watercress,
Four little possums shared a sweet,
Five little possums, pretending to sleep,
Shut their eyes and wouldn't eat.

One little owl played the violin,
Two little owls played the flute,
Three little owls played, "Yankee Doodle,"
Four little owls stayed mute,
Five little owls sang out of tune
And crooned, "We don't give a hoot!"

One little lamb put on records,
Two little lambs put on the light,
Three little lambs put the rug away,
Four little lambs got a fright,
Five little lambs toddled off to bed
And called to the others, "Goodnight!"